WORLD OF NATURE

The Forces of Nature

Philip Jones

Distributed by CHILDRENS PRESS, Chicago

TITLES IN THE SERIES

Face of the Earth
Animals on the Hunt
The Living Ocean
The Forces of Nature

Library of Congress Cataloging in Publication Data

Jones, Philip, Dr.
  The forces of nature

  (World of nature)
  Includes index.
  Summary: Explains and liberally illustrates
variations in weather such as temperature,
seasons, and storms; and delves into volcanic
forces and earthquakes which have helped to
shape the earth.
  1. Weather—Juvenile literature. 2. Earthquakes—Juvenile literature. 3. Volcanoes—
Juvenile literature. [1. Weather. 2. Earthquakes. 3. Volcanoes] I. Title. II. Series:
World of nature (Chicago, Ill.)
QC981.3.J66   551.5   81-38473
ISBN 0-516-00623-1   AACR2

1982 School and Library Edition
Distributed by Childrens Press, Chicago
First published in 1981 by
Wayland Publishers Limited
49 Lansdowne Place, Hove
East Sussex BN3 1HF, England

© Copyright 1981 Wayland Publishers Ltd

Printed in Italy by s.p.a. Sagdos, Milan

Contents

Introduction

This book looks at some of the physical forces of the Earth and atmosphere which affect our lives: the weather, earthquakes and volcanoes.

The Earth is surrounded by a layer of air which we call the atmosphere. The thickness of this layer compared with the size of the Earth is similar to an egg shell compared with the size of an egg. The main force which acts upon the Earth is the sun, whose rays heat up the Earth's land and water surfaces. Without this constant heat there would be no weather or life and the Earth would be a dead planet. The atmosphere moves this heat from the hot equatorial areas to the cold polar regions, and we call the various effects of this constant state of movement the weather.

By far the greatest differences in our weather come from the changes each year which give us the winter, spring, summer and autumn seasons. In summer, temperatures are higher because the days are longer and the sun rises higher above the horizon. In winter, when the days are short and the sun stays low in the sky, temperatures fall. These changes occur at roughly the same time each year and are not unexpected, although some winters are colder than others and some summers warmer than others. Changes in our weather from day to day lead us to ask why there are clouds and rain. Clouds, and the rain they sometimes bring, are carried along by the force of the atmosphere we call the wind. When we can recognize the different types of clouds, we learn that they give an indication of the weather for the next few hours. It is often easy to recognize the types of clouds which lead to rain. The strength of the wind also changes. On some days it is calm or there is only a slight breeze; on others there are gales, storms and hurricane force winds. Very high winds are the most destructive force of the weather. The power involved in hurricanes is difficult to imagine, but the effects are all too evident in the thousands of dead and homeless these storms leave in their path.

The final section of the book moves away from the weather to the forces of Nature that shape the land. Hardly a month passes without the effects of an earthquake or a volcano being reported in the news. These occur as a result of earth movements deep in the earth, usually in well defined areas which are called earthquake-prone regions. Although the violent earth movements which cause these events are almost impossible to predict, the results are very dramatic and some of the pictures in this book were taken in very dangerous conditions.

Wind, Sun and Snow

The powerful force of the weather affects our daily lives. The strong winds and tides of spring and autumn may cause floods which can damage houses and crops. During the summer the sunshine ripens the crops in the fields. Winter brings the snow to cover the ground and protect the seeds from the frost.

typical scene in autumn, with storm-driven waves beating against e coast. Overcast skies bring rain which falls in showers in the rong winds. In between the showers there are sunny intervals.

Crops maturing in a field on a warm summer day. Soon harvest time will arrive and the crops will be gathered. A poor harvest, sometimes due to bad weather, often means there will be food shortages.

scene from the depths of winter. Everything is covered in a thick white blanket of snow. ound the houses some of the snow has been cleared and is piled up. When the snow melts in ng these piles will remain for a while after the rest of the snow has gone.

3

Hot and Cold

Air temperature changes during the year cause us to have the four seasons. winter it is cold and temperatures are low, whereas in summer it is warm they are high. During spring and autumn temperatures are between those winter and summer. The variation in air temperature throughout the year is to the height of the sun above the horizon. In winter the sun is low and o visible for eight hours during the day, while in the summer it is high and visi for sixteen hours. The amount of sunshine determines the average temperature although day-to-day temperatures are affected by the amount of clouds and direction from which the wind is blowing.

In summer we wear fewer clothes. Ice cream and lollipops help to keep us cool.

Average temperature during April: 8°C.

Average temperature during July: 16°C.

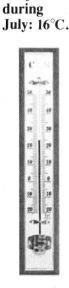

Spring: From March to May, trees blossom and flowers bloom.

In winter it is cold and we wrap ourselves up in woollen scarves, hats and mittens to stay warm.

Summer: From June until August the countryside is coloured all shades of green. The days are long and warm.

Temperatures during the day

Temperatures are warmer during the day than at night. This is because the sun provides light and heat during the day whereas at night there is no sun. These are examples of the temperature variations during a typical summer's day.

Autumn: From September to November leaves begin to change from green to brown.

Average temperature during October: 10°C

Average temperature during January: 4°C

Winter: From December to February of the next year temperatures are cold. Often there is snowfall and ice forms on lakes.

Morning: The sun has raised temperatures during the morning.

Temperature: 12°C

Midday: The sun is at its highest point and it is hot.

Temperature: 25°C

Afternoon: As the sun gradually crosses the horizon temperatures cool.

Temperature: 17°C

Evening: The sun has now disappeared from view. During the night the temperature is at its coldest.

Temperature: 10°C.

The four seasons of the year

Spring. Trees are in blossom, preparing to fruit later. Farmers are sowing the seeds.

Summer. Long, sunny days allow the fruit and crops to mature. Many people take their holidays at this time.

Here we have typical pictures of the four seasons. Of course, they vary from country to country. In Norway and Sweden, for example, winters are long and cold. They start in November and go on until April. Farther south they are shorter and in parts of Spain and southern Italy they are mild and snow rarely falls. Summers are short in Norway and Sweden and long in southern Italy and Spain. The type of weather we have during a particular season depends on where in the world we live. Regions that experience similar types of weather from year to year during the different seasons are said to have the same climate.

Autumn: Vegetation turns from green to warm shades of brown. Crops are harvested.

Vinter: The air is cold and there are often periods cold enough for snow. Here the ground is covered in a white carpet of snow.

The same place in different seasons

In summer the trees and plants are green.

In autumn the leaves turn to reddish-brown.

These pictures show the same area at different times of the year. Here, the changes from one season to the next can be seen easily. In the tropical zones near the equator, however, the differences between seasons are very slight and certain regions have similar weather throughout the year. In some tropical regions the seasons are marked by the onset of heavy rainfall with little change in air temperature. This may be referred to as the rainy season or, in India and South-East Asia, as the monsoon.

...now lies on the ground particularly in the mountains.

Plants and trees begin to grow again with the coming of spring.

The same season in different places

At Okinawa, in the south of Japan, the sea is warm enough for swimming in April.

At Miyazaki in the south of the island of Kyushu, spring is beginning.

At Kochi in the south of the main island Honshu, fruit trees are in blossom.

At Niigata in the north of Honshu, the land is being prepared for rice cultivation. Spring has not yet arrived.

In the northern mountains of Honshu, people are still taking skiing holidays.

In Britain, from the Shetland Isles of Scotland to Land's End in Cornwall, we have great differences in our weather. Average temperatures are 5°C colder in northern Scotland than in southern England. In early spring snow is normally lying in the higher parts of Scotland and over most parts in colder than normal springs, whereas in Devon trees can be in blossom and farmers are beginning to sow seeds. Because of these differences, a greater variety of plants and crops can be grown in southern England than in Scotland. Here we have some examples of weather conditions in towns in Japan during April. Japan, like Britain, is a group of islands which lie roughly in a north-south direction. However, the distance between the northern and southern ends is much greater. Japan, therefore, experiences much greater variations in its weather from place to place at the same time than Britain does. Look up the places on a map of Japan.

Kyoto, in southern Honshu, the trees also blossoming.

At Nagano, in the centre of Honshu, spring has arrived, the trees are bare.

At Tokyo, the capital of Japan, the first new leaves are forming on the trees.

Aomori, in the north of Honshu, snow till lying in the street.

In Hokkaido, the northern island, children can still go sledging.

In the extreme north of Hokkaido the ice covering the sea has only just melted.

11

Above and below the clouds

Here we are in an aeroplane above the clouds, where the air is clear and we can see far into the distance. There is a marked contrast between the clear air above the clouds and the clouds themselves. The surface of the clouds is at roughly the same level throughout the picture. The fluffiness of the surface is formed by wind currents which have a similar effect at sea where they form the waves.

The same clouds seen from below. The mountain disappears into the layer of clouds.

Why are there clouds?

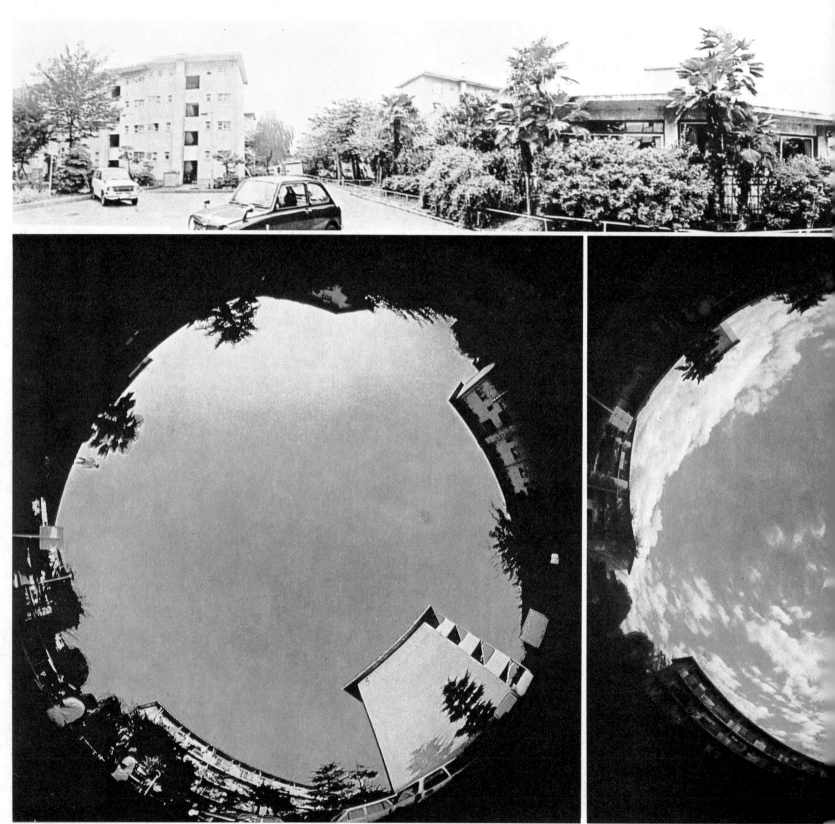

The sky above is almost totally cloudless. During the summer, cloud-free days are the hottest of the entire year. In winter, however, cloud-free days are very cold.

Here the sky is partly covered with cotton-wool-like clouds. These will

Clouds are composed of tiny water droplets or, if the air temperature is cold, crystals of ice. This water has been taken from lakes or the sea by a process called evaporation. The water is in gaseous form, like steam from a kettle, and is called water vapour. When air is forced to rise in order to pass over mountain ranges, the water vapour cannot be held by the cooler air and is condensed into water droplets that make up clouds. Evaporation of water from the Earth's surface is only possible of course where water is available. So it is often cloudy near coasts – cloudless over deserts.

The top picture on these pages is a view looking straight ahead and the others are complete pictures of the sky above, taken in different weather conditions with a special photographic lens.

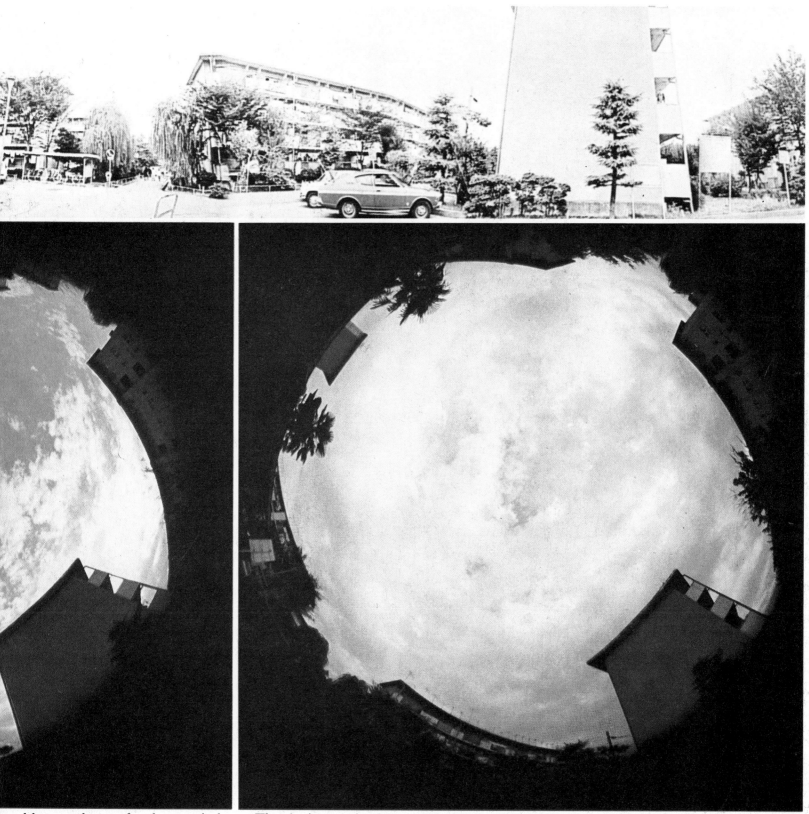

blot out the sun for short periods.

The sky is completely covered with clouds but they are not rain clouds. The air temperature is cooler because of the lack of direct sunlight.

The various types of clouds

Cirrus clouds occur at a great height and appear feathery. They are drawn out into lines by the wind.

Cumulus resemble pieces of cotton wool floating in the sky. The bases of cumulus clouds are flat and their tops shaped like domes.

Cirrocumulus are small, white clouds in lines or ripples rather like the skin of a mackerel.

Altocumulus clouds look like waves on the sea. They usually mean rain.

Stratocumulus are layered clouds. Direct sunlight is cut out by this grey layer.

Nimbostratus is a layer of low, grey cloud from which rain or snow falls continuously.

Clouds occur in many forms at different heights in the sky. Knowledge of the types of clouds and the wind direction allows us to make our first weather forecasts. Rain falls from low clouds such as nimbostratus or cumulonimbus. Cirrus-type clouds give us the first indication that rain is on the way, and these are closely followed by alto-type clouds. The average heights of the various types of cloud are given in the picture below, which represents a slice through the atmosphere.

irrostratus is a whitish sheet of cloud which forms haloes around the sun or moon.

ltostratus is a uniform sheet of grey cloud. It may carry rain.

mulonimbus clouds are associated with heavy rain, thunder and lightning.

ratus is a very low, uniform layer of grey cloud, en low enough to cover small hills.

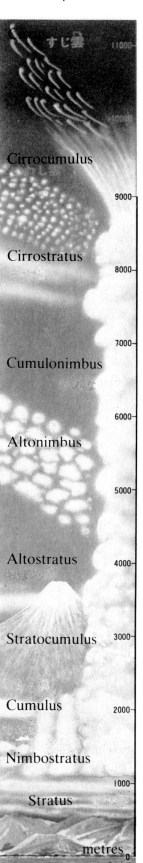

Cirrocumulus

Cirrostratus

Cumulonimbus

Altonimbus

Altostratus

Stratocumulus

Cumulus

Nimbostratus

Stratus

metres

When clouds form at ground level it is called fog. Here is the same stretch of road in both foggy and clear conditions. Fog is dangerous and causes many road accidents.

For centuries we have used the wind to help us in everyday tasks. Windmills harness the wind's energy to grind corn. In parts of the world, particularly the Netherlands, the force of the wind is used to pump water from fields into canals to maintain the best conditions for growing crops. In the future, larger windmills could generate some of our electricity.

The four pictures show the differing strength of the wind: 1. The air is calm and the tree is motionless; 2. A light breeze rustles through the leaves; 3. The wind is fresh and small branches are swaying in the wind; 4. The wind is of gale force and the whole tree is in motion.

The direction of the wind: If the flag is upright on one side of the mast then the wind is blowing from the opposite side.

Snow

The same scene during summer.

Prolonged snowfall has covered the area in a white blanket. The flakes of snow distort the rays of light and make the picture indistinct and blurred.

Snow is the form in which rain falls when the air temperature is below the freezing point of water. Snow is therefore frequent in places which experience freezing conditions during winter. As air temperatures cool at higher altitudes, snow is common in most mountainous regions of the world, where it is often very deep.

The depth of accumulated snow is revealed in this picture of a road cleared by a snowplough.

In the lower picture the roof is being swept to reduce the weight of snow on it.

Different forms of snow

Wet snow

Snowfall occurring at temperatures very near to freezing point is usually wet snow. Snow at these temperatures easily binds together to form snowmen and snowballs. This type of snow is very dangerous for traffic as it compacts to slippery ice. Salt is put on the roads to break up the ice. This type of snow is the most common in Britain.

Wet snow has collected on these trees. The branches bend under the weight of the snow.

Some snow has collected on these telegraph wires, which, as the temperature has dropped, has frozen and covered the wires in ice.

After a fall of snow this old tree trunk looks as if it has a crown of snow on it.

If you make a snowball and roll it downhill, it will become bigger and bigger.

Children are making a snowman while the snow is still quite fresh.

owdery snow

en snow falls at temperatures much below freezing point the snow-
kes are powdery and small. The snow will not bind together as wet
w does, and it does not turn to ice on roads. This type of snowfall is
e in Britain and is more typical of polar and mountainous regions.

y snow is blown by the winds on this mountainside. The wind can blow
w into deep drifts in sheltered spots.

wdery snow is the best for skiing. Skiing conditions change according
the type of snow on the mountainside.

The thaw

In spring when the temperature rises, the snow melts or
thaws. The water forms little streams and the remaining
snow is often sculptured into odd shapes.

The snow turns to water and this seeps through the soil
or is channelled to a stream.

In wooded areas, the snow melts more rapidly than in
the surrounding country.

31

Snow crystals

Ice crystals join together to form flakes of snow. Each snow crystal is different from every other, although many of the designs are similar. These pictures show some of the shapes as they are seen under a microscope.

At temperatures slightly above the freezing point of water the flakes partially melt and tend to stick together to form larger ones. This type of snow is easily compacted to ice.

These snow crystals are from powdery, dry snow which falls at temperatures below the freezing point of water. It does not compact or bind as wet snow and is therefore less of a hazard to traffic. The density of snow is much less than water and the depth of a fall of snow is roughly equivalent to ten times that of the same amount of water.

ost snow crystals are star-shaped and tend to be six-sided. Under a microscope it is possible to the incredibly detailed, regular structure of each flake.

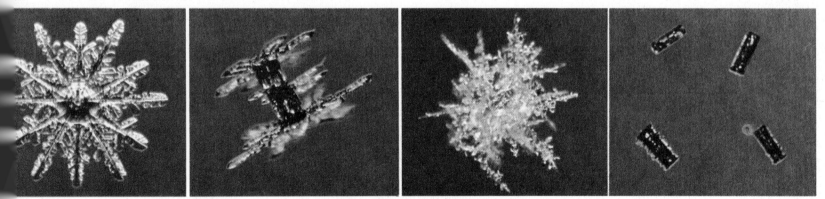

ne irregular forms of snow crystals. Here we have a star with twelve points; an odd-shaped stal which looks like a racing car; some shoots jutting out at all angles from a central cluster; some little rectangular blocks.

Ice

During winter, in many parts of the world, the air temperature is low enough for lakes and rivers to freeze, covering the water with a layer of ice. If the winter is very cold, the ice will be sufficiently thick for people to walk and skate on it. Only small rivers freeze completely and normally the water beneath the ice allows fish and other animals to survive. In polar regions the temperatures are cold enough for large areas of the sea to freeze over.

On a river, ice forms first of all near the banks rather than in the fast-moving water.

The lake during summer, boats can move freely.

Ice has formed over the lake, stopping boats travelling across it.

On the sea, ice forms these pancake patterns before it spreads into an ice sheet.

A winter experiment

During a cold winter's night you can make some ice by leaving some water outside on an old pane of glass. In the morning the water will have solidified forming a thin layer of ice on the glass. In the ice you will be able to see lines of ice crystals.

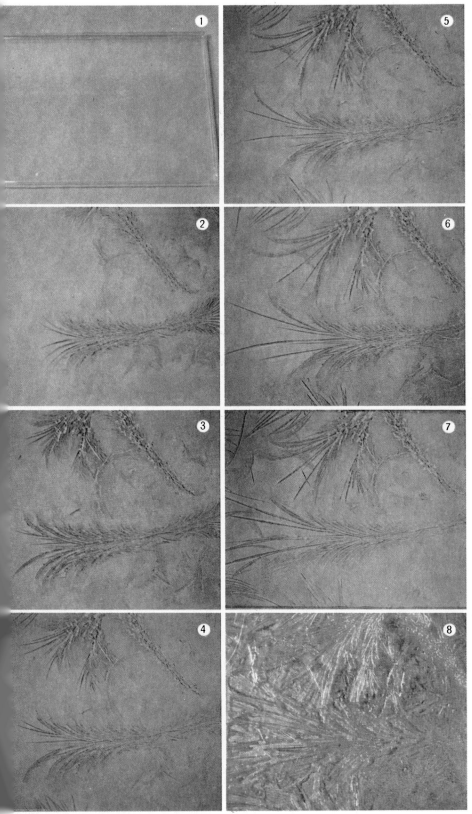

Skating on a frozen lake. Notice the scratches on the ice caused by the blades of the skates.

These eight pictures show the gradual formation of ice on a sheet of glass. The colder it is the quicker the ice forms.

The ice which has formed on this lake is being cut for some use. Further ice will form on the lake in due course.

Icicles and frost

Icicles

All forms of water freeze when the temperature cools below freezing point. Icicles and frost are both different forms of frozen water.

Water which is alternately freezing and melting forms icicles, sometimes of the most fantastic shapes.

Here the sun melts some of the snow on a roof. The water runs down to the shady eaves and freezes to form icicles.

Rain and snow have collected on this tree, melted in sunlight and then refrozen at night.

These icicles have been formed by a freezing waterfall. Snow has fallen later and this has helped add to the size of the icicles.

Ice designs on windows

Frost

Minute ice crystals form on a window during long cold winter nights. Each leaf-like pattern is unique.

When air temperatures cool at night during winter, water vapour in the air is deposited as dew. This freezes to form ice particles or frost.

e beautiful ice patterns on windows. It's difficult to believe it's frozen water!

Frost forms quickly on soft, damp ground. If you walk on frosty ground, you can hear the ice crystals crunching underfoot.

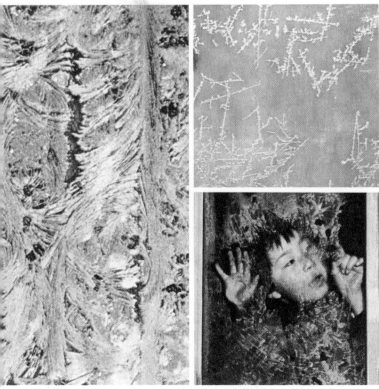

designs of ice on windows can be very intricate. Sometimes the unt of ice on a window can cause the glass to break.

The topmost water in the soil has frozen due to the cold conditions.

The icy countryside

Trees of ice

In mountainous and polar regions the winters are hard and severe. Temperatures even during the daytime are never above freezing point. Ice and frost form on everything which is not covered by snow. A deep snow cover protects the plants from the harshness of the winter.

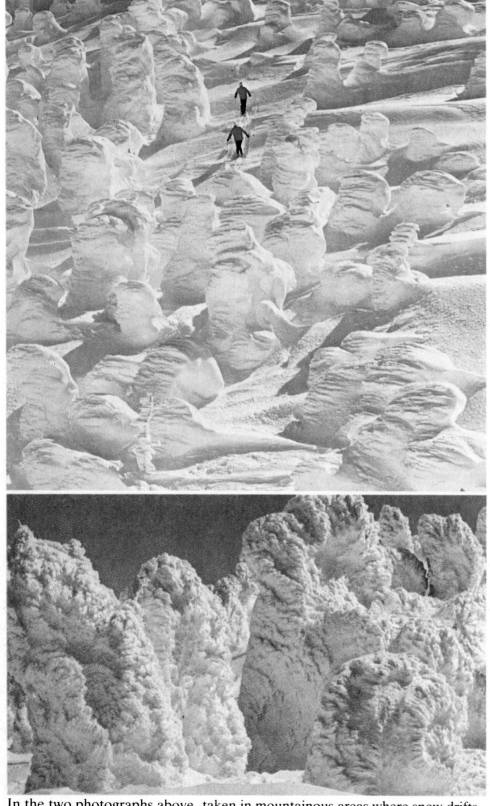

In the two photographs above, taken in mountainous areas where snow drifts, the weird shapes are trees covered with snow which has turned to ice as the winter became colder.

Ice has covered these trees completely.

More frost

In winter the effects of frost can be severe. Many plants die. Under snow, ground temperatures are only just below freezing, but without this cover they can be -50°C or even colder. In parts of eastern Siberia it is so cold that all the soil is frozen completely.

Frost has formed in this field. Only trees and plants able to withstand these extreme temperatures will survive to the next spring.

Frost has coated these pine cones . . .

. . .formed in cracks on this wooden bridge . . .

. . .frozen this ground hard.

A swirl of clouds

Off Japan in the Pacific Ocean, a swirl of storm clouds approaches the southern coast. This is an artist's impression of a typhoon viewed from space. Satellites have been launched into space especially to take pictures which will help with weather forecasting. Warning of the typhoon can now be given to those living in the path of the storm before it hits them. The clear, central part of the typhoon called the 'eye', is an area of relatively light winds. The greatest wind speeds are immediately around the eye; they decrease again towards the edges of the swirl.

The strength of the wind

When the wind blows in polar regions the powdery snow is lifted from the ground and causes a blizzard.

The wind drives the sea into waves. In strong winds the tops of the waves are broken off into a spray of water droplets which will lash against passing ships.

The speed of the wind can be measured with instruments or judged by the movements of trees and flags. At sea the wind forms the waves at the surface and the stronger the wind the larger and more dangerous the waves. The wind can drive the sea over the beach, lashing sea-fronts with huge waves. Low-lying coastal regions, such as parts of the Netherlands, can be flooded. Inland, when wind speeds increase to severe gales, roofs may be ripped off houses, and telegraph and electricity cables pulled down.

e giant funnel of cloud is a whirling mass of air known as a tornado, the st violent kind of wind there is. Luckily tornadoes are small, but they l lift up cars, animals and people, uproot trees, and toss them all aside f they were matchsticks.

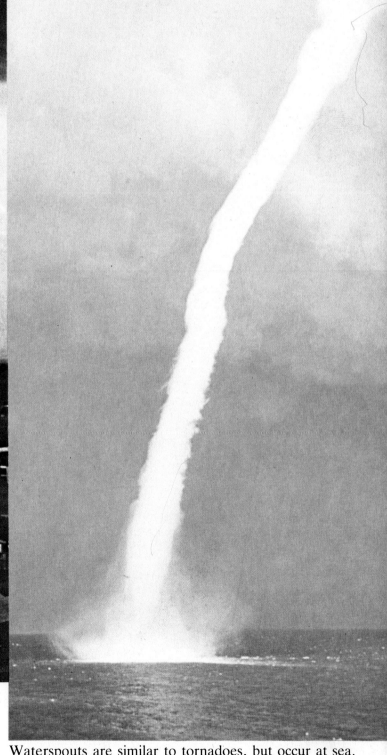

Waterspouts are similar to tornadoes, but occur at sea. The whirling columns of air suck up water, and sometimes fish, landing them some distance away.

Thunder and lightning

Cirrus clouds give an indication of the coming rain.

The clouds are gathering ready for the storm.

The city is covered in a dark, menacing cloud. Thunder may be heard in the distance. Heavy rain (or hail) begins to fall. When the storm centre is near, lightning is seen as electric charges are transferred from the cloud to the ground. The lightning flash momentarily releases much heat which suddenly expands the air. The air contracts immediately after the flash and this causes a clap, or claps, of thunder.

Lightning strikes! A building's conductor will take the electric charge.

A tree struck by a fork of lightning.

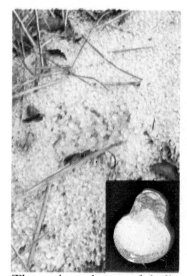

There is a layer of hailstones − pellets of ice − on the ground. Each hailstone is formed in layers; you can see them if you cut a hailstone in half. Large hailstones do much damage to crops and to buildings such as greenhouses.

Violent storms

Storm-driven waves break with fury on coastal sea defences, threatening houses.

Hurricanes, typhoons and cyclones are different names for violent, revolving storms which develop over warmer areas of the tropical oceans. The evaporation of sea water forms masses of clouds and this releases heat to the air, providing sufficient energy to drive the storm. Until recently, prediction of such storms was not possible, but now satellites give us an early warning of their approach and attempts can be made to direct a storm away from populated areas.

The swirl of clouds circle the 'eye' — the calm centre — of the storm. The storms are known as hurricanes in the Atlantic and eastern Pacific Oceans, typhoons in the western Pacific, and cyclones in the Indian Ocean.

Continuous rain for many days has lead to serious flooding in this American town.

White death

Snow covers this mountain valley during winter, making a very picturesque scene. However, there is danger from avalanches occurring on the valley side. The inset picture is the same area in the summer.

An avalanche is a mass of snow which slides into flat valleys from the valley slopes, causing great destruction. Parts of towns or villages may be buried. Avalanches are caused when the snow becomes detached from the ground beneath it and begins to slide. They may be triggered off by a skier or by the melting of snow in spring. Dogs have been trained to find people buried by avalanches, as it is possible to survive for a short time under the snow.

ere is little to indicate that an avalanche is about commence.

e avalanche is just beginning. The ground has en revealed beneath the snow.

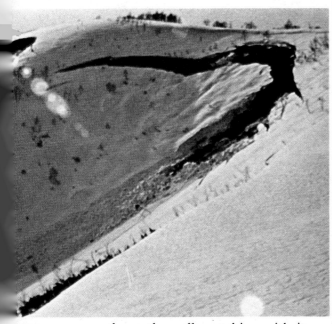

snow moves down the valley, taking with it e trees and probably some loose rocks.

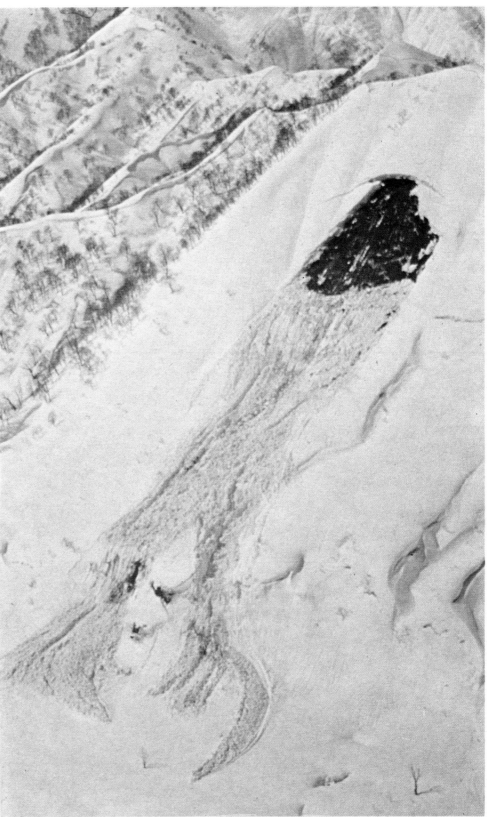

The avalanche is over, leaving its traces clearly visible. On this occasion no-one has been injured.

The formation of the Earth

When you look at a map of the world, the continents of Africa and South America look like pieces of a jigsaw puzzle. If you cut roughly around the outline of the continents, not forgetting Antarctica, they match up quite well. North America joins to North Africa, Antarctica wedges between south-eastern Africa and southern Australia, and India, separated from the rest of Asia, fits between East Africa and Antarctica. Everything fits together remarkably well and confirms the fact that our continents, now great distances apart, were, millions of years ago, all one piece of land.

Geological evidence suggests that 200 million years ago there was only one very large continent, surrounded by ocean. This single continent has been called Pangaea. Since that time, movements within the earth, which we see on the surface as earthquakes and volcanoes, have caused pieces of that continent to break off and drift apart. These pieces are our present-day continents. This movement is still continuing but it is very, very slow − a continent would take thirty years to move from the top to the bottom of this page. Not all continents move as much as others. Europe, for example, has remained in more or less the same position during the last 200 million years.

Movement of the continents is often forced by new ocean floor being created between continents by underwater volcanoes. This is the case with the American and the African continents. At certain points in the Atlantic Ocean there are volcanic islands: Iceland and the Azores in the north Atlantic, and St Helena and Tristan da Cunha in the south Atlantic. These islands were all formed by volcanic activity and are roughly in the centre of the ocean. The creation of new ocean floor is called sea-floor spreading.

Elsewhere, the sea floor is being absorbed slowly back into the earth. For example, the Pacific Ocean is gradually becoming smaller. The places where the continents join under the ocean, the areas where new ocean floor is made and where it is reabsorbed, are the main areas of earthquake and volcanic activity. These regions form a ring around the Pacific Coast, the Mid-Atlantic Ridge and on a line joining the Mediterranean to South-East Asia. Away from these areas, volcanoes are few and any earthquakes that occur generally pass unnoticed.

When continents move towards each other, the rocks between the two are forced upwards to become vast mountain ranges. India broke away from the side of Africa and moved north into the vast continent of Asia. As this occurred, the Himalayan mountain range was formed by many severe earthquakes over millions of years. Similarly, as Africa nudged towards Europe, the Alps were formed in Europe and the Atlas mountain range in north-west Africa. Again, the process was slow and is still continuing slowly. This process is termed 'mountain building.' The Mediterranean area is a major earthquake zone and many towns and cities have been destroyed by earthquakes in Italy, Yugoslavia and Greece in Europe, and in Algeria in North Africa. There are also a number of volcanoes in southern parts of Italy.

Our Earth is therefore in a continual state of evolution and has been since its formation. The movement is slow and gradual, and it takes millions of years before significant changes to the world are noticeable. Nothing to change the map will affect the Earth in our lifetimes. Although earthquakes and volcanoes appear to occur without warning, studies in different years suggest that there are periods when there are fewer, and periods when there are more earthquakes and volcanoes. In the years between 1920 and 1950 there were fewer earthquakes and volcanic eruptions recorded, but in recent years there have been more. Whether this trend will continue or not, we can only wait and see.

olten rock cascades from the mouth of a volcano.

Inside the Earth

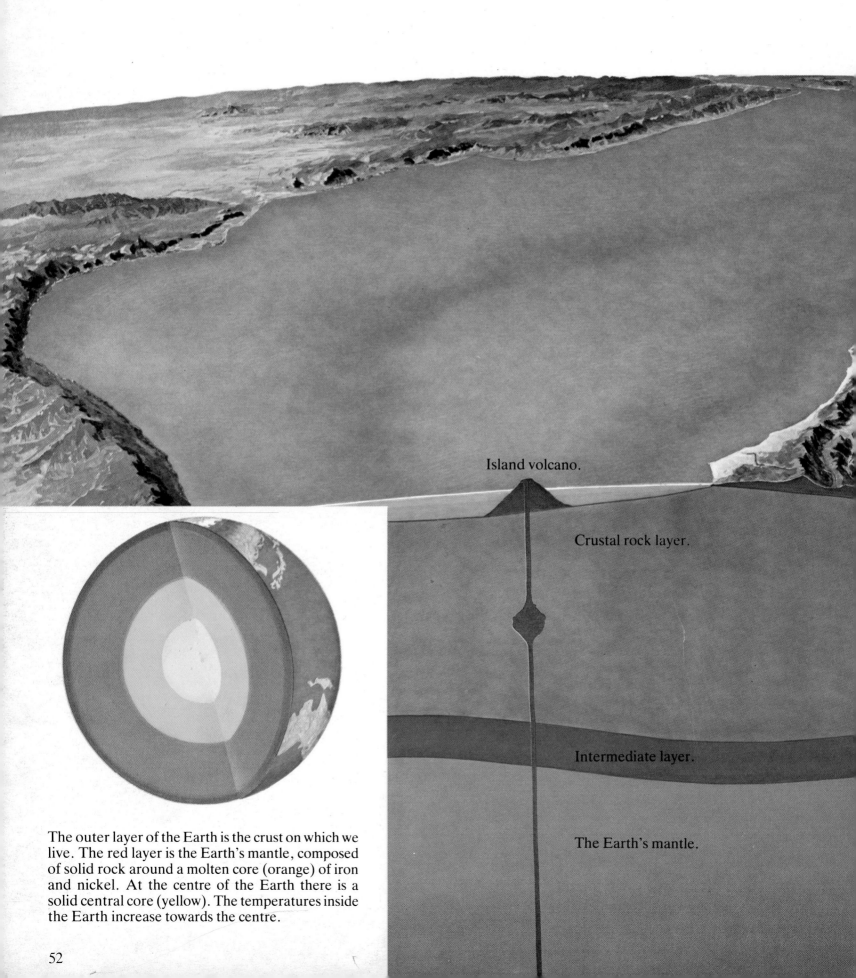

Island volcano.

Crustal rock layer.

Intermediate layer.

The Earth's mantle.

The outer layer of the Earth is the crust on which we live. The red layer is the Earth's mantle, composed of solid rock around a molten core (orange) of iron and nickel. At the centre of the Earth there is a solid central core (yellow). The temperatures inside the Earth increase towards the centre.

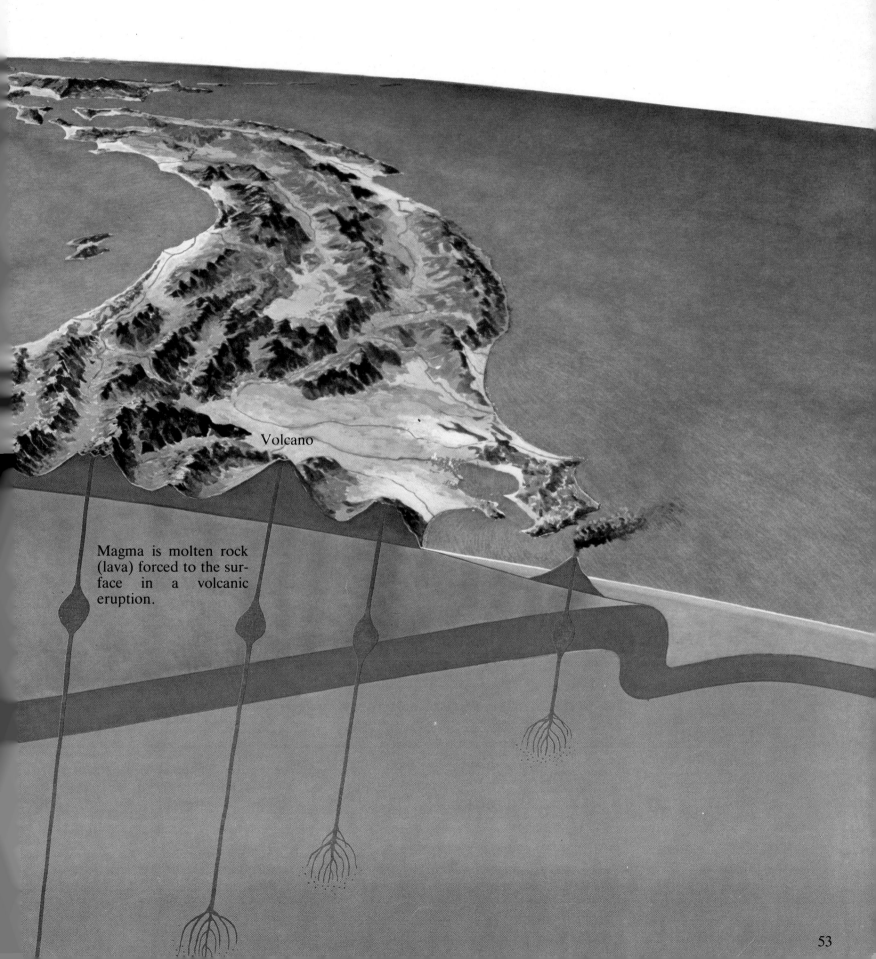

This part of the Earth's crust has been sliced through to reveal the structure beneath the surface. We can see that the volcanoes are connected to molten rock at great depths in the Earth. Volcanoes tend to occur in certain regions of the world where the crust is unstable. Pressures and forces from inside the Earth cause volcanoes to erupt and little is known as to why this happens or if the processes can be predicted in advance.

Volcano

Magma is molten rock (lava) forced to the surface in a volcanic eruption.

Volcanic eruptions

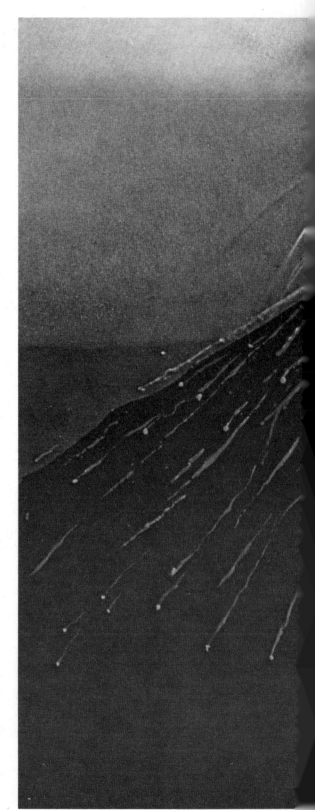

At the start of a volcanic eruption clouds of ash, larger particles, smoke and fumes are ejected from the volcanic cone.

Geological evidence suggests that there have been about 800 different volcanoes which have erupted at some time. Some erupt frequently, some occasionally and others have erupted only once in recorded history. Many volcanoes are classed as dormant; that is, they have erupted in the past but this may have been millions of years ago and only the characteristic cone-shaped mountains remains. The volcanic cone is not always present at the surface. The force of the eruption may have been so violent as to cause the walls of the cone to collapse inwards, leaving a crater which is known as a caldera. In time and if there is no more volcanic activity, this crater will solidify and water will collect in it to form a lake.

The type of eruption will also vary from volcano to volcano. However, there are many similar features between eruptions of the same volcano at different times. Eruptions can be explosive, as in the example here, with near molten rock hurled great distances from the volcano and giant clouds of ash forced to great heights in the atmosphere. This ash often darkens the sky by blocking out the sun's light and can travel vast distances when blown along by the wind. When a volcanic eruption occurred in Iceland in 1783, ash from the cone was reported as falling in Scotland. Compared with this explosive type, other eruptions are minor, with little explosive activity. In some, continuous streams of molten rock, known as lava, flow from the volcano.

Apart from the ejection of molten lava, rock and ash particles, large amounts of gases are released into the atmosphere. Much of this is steam which is formed when water comes into contact with the molten rock. Other gases are released directly by the volcano, including nitrogen, sulphur dioxide and hydrogen sulphide. These last two explain the pungent smell which is very evident in a region after a volcanic eruption.

Near molten pieces of rock are hurled from the volcano. These rain down the side of the crater and often precede the flow of molten lava from the central cone or a weak point in the side of the cone.

After the initial explosive stage of a volcanic eruption, some volcanoes calm down to stay quiet for periods which range from a few days to millions of years. The majority move into the second stage of an eruption when a river, or rivers, of molten lava flows from the centre or the side of the volcano. Some volcanoes may pass straight to this second stage. Most volcanoes have a long history extending back over thousands or millions of years. Over this period the cone is built up by many stratified layers of lava. Each fresh eruption pro-

Rivers of lava, clouds of ash

A great cloud of smoke and ash has been ejected from the volcano and many minor earthquakes accompany the eruption. Later, molten lava will flow down the mountainside.

A volcano at sea. An earlier eruption may have formed the island itself. Many islands, particularly around the coast of the Pacific Ocean, have been formed by volcanic action.

duces at least one new layer. In some volcanoes, vast areas around the volcano are covered by the lava and this solidifies on cooling. Lava is rarely dangerous as it moves relatively slowly, enabling people to be evacuated, although property and vegetation in the lava path will be destroyed.

The most dangerous phase of a volcanic eruption is the initial, explosive stage, partly because it occurs without any warning. There have been many famous volcanic eruptions in the past and probably the most famous is that of Mt Vesuvius, near Naples in Italy, in A.D. 79. The entire city of Pompeii and neighbouring towns of Herculaneum and Stabiae were buried in ash, killing all those unable to escape quickly enough. The ash preserved the city. Excavation has revealed the city beneath the ash, with bodies lying almost intact where they fell, and has given us an unparalleled look back at the past. Mt Vesuvius has erupted many times since that time but never with such dramatic effect.

By far the most explosive volcano of recent times occurred on the island of Krakatoa between the Indonesian islands of Java and Sumatra in August, 1883. (Look up the island on a map to get an idea of how far the effects were felt from the island.) The island itself completely disappeared under the sea, together with the entire population. Enormous tidal waves or *tsunamis* overwhelmed settlements on shore lines around the Pacific and a total of 35,000 people were killed, mostly by the tidal wave. The tidal wave was as high as a ten-storey building and the wave was felt off Cape Horn, on the extreme tip of South America, half-way around the world! The sound of the eruption was heard in south-eastern Australia! Vast quantities of dust were ejected into the upper atmosphere where it cannot be reached by clouds nor washed out by rain. This dust stays there for up to seven years before gradually returning to earth. The effect of this dust scatters and cuts out some of the rays of sunlight. For a number of years afterwards, the world experienced some wonderful sunsets, many of which have been painted by artists of the time.

During the 1920s further volcanic activity took place beneath the sea in the area and a new island was formed in the same position as the old. The island was named by those living on neighbouring islands: Anak Krakatoa — son of Krakatoa.

A river of lava flowing down the side of Mount Etna, Sicily.

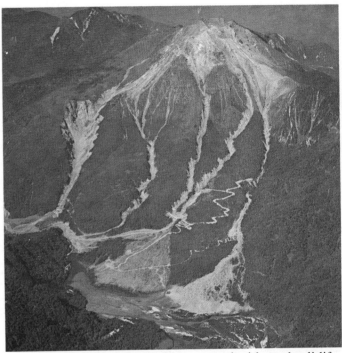

Rivers of lava flow down this mountainside and solidify on meeting the stream at the bottom.

Gases emitted by some volcanoes kill plants by smothering them in toxic fumes

Trees and other vegetation are burnt to ashes when they come in contact with the lava flow.

A volcano starts to erupt at sea, sending jets of boiling water into the air.

Living with volcanoes

Lava from the erupting volcano has fortunately missed the town in the foreground. Instead the lava has flowed down to the sea, causing clouds of steam.

Lava advances on the remains of this building, which has been abandoned by its occupants.

Millions of people have lost their lives after volcanic eruptions and entire civilizations have been destroyed, but many still continue to live near active volcanoes. Why should this be? The land near a volcano becomes covered in ash, which mixes with the soil and produces fertile agricultural land. People living near volcanoes have, therefore decided, that the benefits to agriculture outweigh the disastrous effects of an occasional eruption.

Volcanic ash has, in some cases, completely buried the houses in this town in Iceland. Although the inhabitants have escaped, their homes will probably be destroyed.

Near molten boulders, rocks and ash are ejected from the volcano (top picture). These have landed at the base of the volcano (bottom picture) and many houses, and the vegetation, have been destroyed.

The earth trembles

The force of an earthquake has caused this road to break up.

The result of a minor earth tremor.

Earthquakes occur along lines of possible earth movement known as fault planes. The two sides of the fault are attempting to slide past each other and the stresses which build up are released, so causing the earthquake. We are only aware of the most severe earthquakes, and these tend to occur together with volcanoes in fairly clearly defined regions. Despite this, and much scientific research, it is still proving very difficult to predict earthquakes accurately. Even when earthquakes occur at sea their effects are often felt on land by destructive waves called *tsunamis*, or tidal waves.

When this picture was taken the beach was quiet. The sea was calm.

The *tsunami* or tidal wave arrives on the beach, travelling at speeds of up to 40 km/h (25mph).

The beach is destroyed and debris floats in the angry water. This tidal wave occurred in Japan where they are most frequent. This is why we use the Japanese word *tsunami*.

Earthquakes and destruction

Managua, the capital of Nicaragua, before and after a recent earthquake.

Although an earthquake generally lasts for less than a minute, it can be very destructive. Buildings and bridges collapse and parts of cities are reduced to rubble. Thousands of people may die as a result of the falling buildings, gas explosions and flooding from burst water pipes. Afterwards, the survivors have to be cared for and essential services, particularly fresh water, must be provided. In earthquake-prone regions buildings are designed to withstand minor shocks. However, despite improvements in design which have saved countless thousands of lives, a major earthquake often destroys a city.

This building's foundations have collapsed and it has fallen on its side.

Organized groups search for possible survivors among the remains of the houses.

The earthquake has caused this bridge to fall on to the road below.

Index